This BASICS book
belongs to

....

....

....

USA

The World

The Galaxy

The Universe

First Aladdin Books edition 1991

First published in 1990 by David Bennett Books Limited
94 Victoria Street, St Albans, Herts AL1 3TG, England

Series Editor: Ruth Thomson
Consultants: Basil Lindsey, M.SC.,Ph.D., M.I. Biol., Principal
Lecturer in Applied Biology, Brighton College of Technology,
Brighton, England and Samuel Taylor, Ph.D., Biology Director,
The New York Hall of Science, New York

Aladdin Books
Macmillan Publishing Company
866 Third Avenue
New York, NY 10022

Printed in Hong Kong

1 2 3 4 5 6 7 8 9 10

Library of Congress Cataloging–in–Publication Data
Wood, Jenny.
Under the sea / written by Jenny Wood: illustrated by Malcolm
Livingstone. —1st Aladdin Books ed.
p. cm. —(Aladdin basics)
Includes index.
Summary: A submarine voyage reveals the secrets of the deep.
including sharks, whales, a coral reef, shipwrecks, and marine
pollution.
ISBN 0-689-71488-2
1. Marine biology—Juvenile literature. 2. Fishes, Deep–sea—
Juvenile literature. 3. Ocean—Juvenile literature. [1. Marine
biology. 2. Fishes. 3. Ocean. 4. Underwater exploration.]
I. Livingstone, Malcolm, ill. II. Title. III. Series.
QH91.16.W66 1991
574.92—dc20 91–7484 CIP AC

Under the sea

Written by
Jenny Wood

Illustrated by
Malcolm Livingstone

Aladdin Books
Macmillan Publishing Company
New York

Maxwell Macmillan International Publishing Group
New York   Oxford   Singapore   Sydney

Long ago, before anybody had invented submarines,
no one knew what was under the sea.
Sailors told terrifying tales of horrible sea monsters
lurking beneath the waves.

We know a lot more about the sea now,
because we can travel below the surface
in underwater boats, called submarines.
A submarine is built strongly. It has to be.
The deeper we go, the more the water will press
on the outside. If the submarine isn't strong
enough, it'll be scrunched into a ball!

We can't tell by looking at it,
but seawater doesn't taste like the water
from your tap. It's salty.

Just look at those fish around us.
Most fish live near the surface
of the sea where there is plenty
of light and food.
Some eat plankton, tiny animals
and plants which drift in the water.
Some eat other fish or sea animals.

Look out! Jellyfish ahead!
They have a nasty sting.

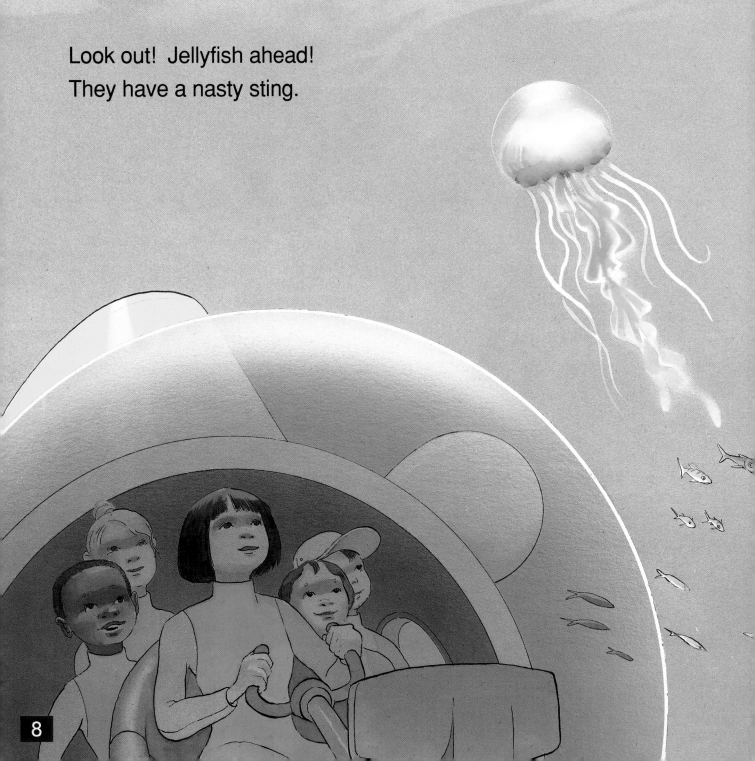

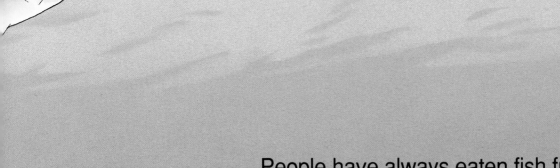

People have always eaten fish from the sea.
Some fishermen use nets, which trail behind
their boats as they move through the water.
When a net is full, it is pulled in
and the fish are unloaded on deck.
Then it's off to market!

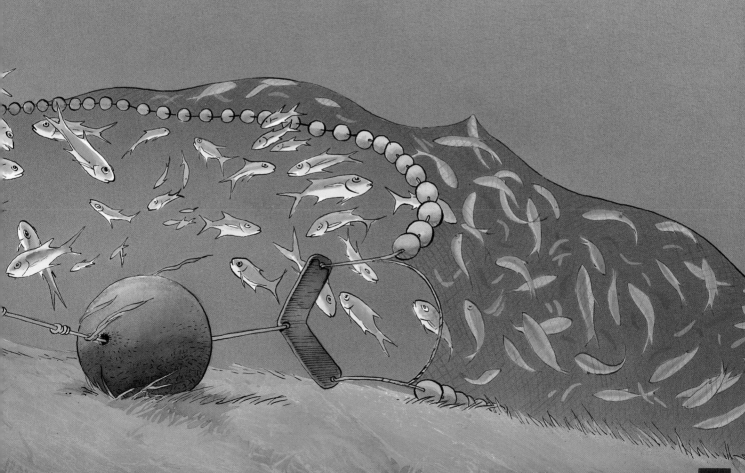

That huge creature whizzing past us
is a hungry tiger shark! Those dolphins
and that turtle had better beware.
Some sharks eat only fish, but the tiger shark
will eat almost anything!

There's gas under the sea bed. Most of this is used in our homes for cooking or heating.

What are these? They're the legs of an oil rig!
People must be drilling for oil here.
In some places there's a lot of oil under the sea.
Special drills from the oil rig cut through
the sea bed to where the oil is.
The oil is then pumped through
pipes all the way back to land.

Yuk! The sea is so dirty here,
the fish have all died.
Some people don't care about the sea.
They dump all kinds of garbage and poisons
into it. This kills the fish and plants.
It's time everybody began to look after the sea
properly. Fortunately, some people are already trying.

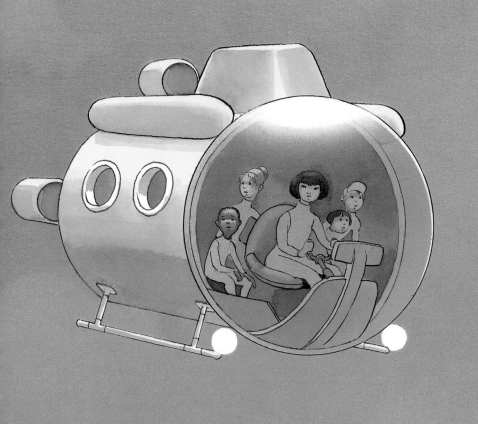

The baby whale must be tired.
Its mother is giving it
a piggyback ride!

That's better! The sea is much cleaner here.
The water is cold, but these humpback whales don't
mind. Whales have a thick layer of fat
called blubber beneath their skin,
which helps keep them warm.

Brrr! We're almost at the North Pole.
The water is so cold here that the surface of the sea
has frozen over. Seals need air to breathe,
so they knock breathing holes through the thin ice.

Tiny sea urchins and red starfish feed
on the seals' droppings.

When people dive under water, they have to carry
tanks of air on their backs to help them breathe.
They also have to wear masks
or helmets, diving suits, and flippers.
Some divers want to learn more about the plants,
fish, and animals which live in the sea.
Others study shipwrecks. Come on,
let's see if we can find a hidden treasure!

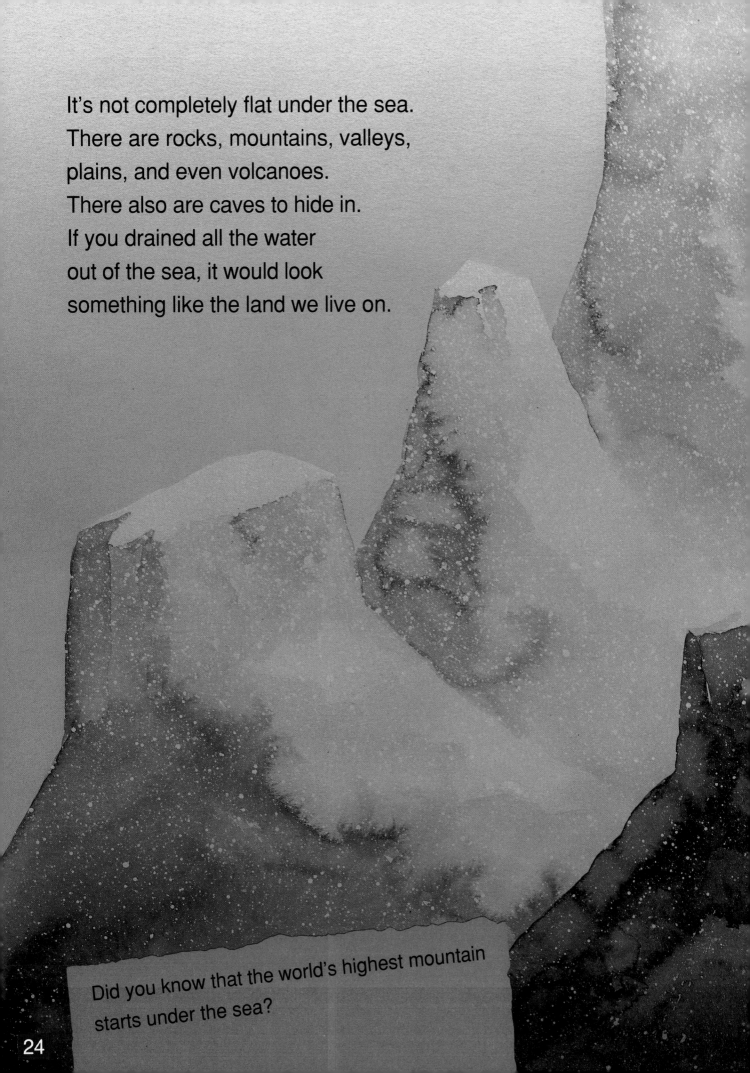

It's not completely flat under the sea.
There are rocks, mountains, valleys,
plains, and even volcanoes.
There also are caves to hide in.
If you drained all the water
out of the sea, it would look
something like the land we live on.

Did you know that the world's highest mountain starts under the sea?

Time to switch on the powerful lights and dive
to the deepest part of the sea.

The sun's warm rays can't reach
to the bottom here. The water is dark and cold.
Most of the fish that live here are hunters.
They have sharp teeth!

The angler fish has a light
which hangs over its mouth.
The light attracts other fish,
which are then gobbled up
by the angler!

Most gulper eels don't have their own light.
They swim along ready to gobble up
anything that comes by!

Let's visit a coral reef on our way back to the surface.
Coral reefs are found in shallow water
in some of the world's warm seas.
Corals are creatures.

Thousands of them live together in huge groups,
which look like mounds, plates, or branches.
They look more like rocks or plants
than animals.

Many colorful fish live around coral reefs,
where there is plenty of light and food.

Here we are just below the surface.
Our underwater journey is over.

INDEX

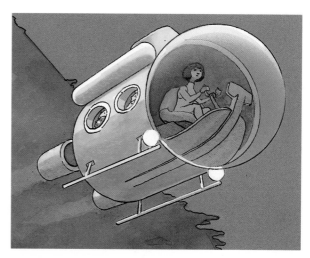

BASICS

An introduction to our world